DISCOVERING
THE UNITED STATES

# Michigan

BY IB LARSEN

**Kids Core**

An Imprint of Abdo Publishing
abdobooks.com

# abdobooks.com

Published by Abdo Publishing, a division of ABDO, PO Box 398166, Minneapolis, Minnesota 55439. Copyright © 2025 by Abdo Consulting Group, Inc. International copyrights reserved in all countries. No part of this book may be reproduced in any form without written permission from the publisher. Kids Core™ is a trademark and logo of Abdo Publishing.

Printed in the United States of America, North Mankato, Minnesota.
052024
092024

Cover Photo: Dennis MacDonald/Shutterstock Images
Interior Photos: AP Images, 4–5; Jukka Jantunen/Shutterstock Images, 7 (top left); Chris Dale/Shutterstock Images, 7 (top right); Shutterstock Images, 7 (bottom left), 7 (bottom right), 9, 24, 26, 28 (top right); iStockphoto, 10; Darlene Stanley/Shutterstock Images, 12–13; Ruslan Maiborodin/Shutterstock Images, 14; Shawshots/Alamy, 16; Jeff Kowalsky/AFP/Getty Images, 18; Leonid Andronov/Shutterstock Images, 20–21, 28 (bottom left); Oleksandr Koretskyi/Shutterstock Images, 23, 28 (bottom right); Red Line Editorial, 28 (top left), 29

Editor: Laura Stickney
Series Designer: Katharine Hale

Library of Congress Control Number: 2023949349

Publisher's Cataloging-in-Publication Data

Names: Larsen, Ib, author.
Title: Michigan / by Ib Larsen
Description: Minneapolis, Minnesota: Abdo Publishing, 2025 | Series: Discovering the United States | Includes online resources and index.
Identifiers: ISBN 9781098293925 (lib. bdg.) | ISBN 9798384913191 (ebook)
Subjects: LCSH: U.S. states--Juvenile literature. | Michigan--History--Juvenile literature. | Midwest States--Juvenile literature. | Physical geography--United States--Juvenile literature.
Classification: DDC 973--dc23

All population data taken from:
"Estimates of Population by Sex, Race, and Hispanic Origin: April 1, 2020 to July 1, 2022." *US Census Bureau, Population Division*, June 2023, census.gov.

# CONTENTS

The Michigan Wolverines' 1969 win over the Ohio Buckeyes led to a new rivalry between the two teams. People called it the Ten Year War.

# CHAPTER 1

# The Great Rivalry

It was November 22, 1969. More than 100,000 people packed Michigan Stadium in Ann Arbor, Michigan. They were there to watch a college football game between the Ohio State Buckeyes and the University of Michigan Wolverines.

The teams had been rivals for decades. But nobody expected this game to be historic. The Buckeyes had won every game of their season. The Wolverines had two losses and a new coach. Most people thought the Buckeyes' winning streak would continue.

The game started. Fullback Jim Otis scored the first touchdown for Ohio State. But then the Wolverines made a run of their own and scored a touchdown too. By halftime, the Wolverines were winning with a score of 24–12. In the second half of the game, each team's defense kept the other team from scoring. The Wolverines won the game.

The 1969 game remains one of the most memorable games in the rivalry. The Buckeyes

# Michigan Facts

**STATE BIRD**

American robin

**STATE TREE**

White pine

**STATE FLOWER**

Apple blossom

**STATE FISH**

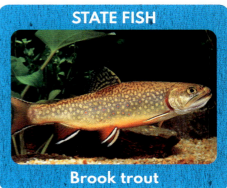

Brook trout

Each US state has a different population, size, and capital city. States also have state symbols.

and Wolverines still face off once a year. It is one of the largest sporting events in Michigan. Each year, the game attracts more than 100,000 people.

# Michigan's Land

Michigan is in the Midwest region of the United States. The state borders Indiana and Ohio to the south. Wisconsin lies to the west. To the north and east is Canada.

Michigan has a unique shape. It is split into two pieces by Lake Michigan and Lake Huron. These pieces are known as the Upper and

## The Great Lakes

The Great Lakes are five large lakes between the United States and Canada. They are named Superior, Michigan, Huron, Erie, and Ontario. Michigan is the only state that borders four of the Great Lakes. Because of this, people call Michigan the Great Lakes State.

Many areas in Michigan's Upper Peninsula, such as Mackinac Island, are known for having mild weather in the summer.

Lower **Peninsulas**. The state is also bordered by Lake Superior and Lake Erie.

Michigan's land includes grasslands and forests. Sugar maple, beech, hemlock, and white pine trees grow in the forests. There are many bodies of water in Michigan too. These include lakes, swamps, and rivers. Fish such as trout, whitefish, and bass swim in these waters.

In winter, Michigan's Upper Peninsula often gets heavier snowfall than the Lower Peninsula.

# Climate

Michigan has four seasons. Snow falls in the winter. By spring, the snow melts. Temperatures rise in the summer.

The Great Lakes affect the state's weather. Water doesn't change temperature as quickly as air. So the lakes cool the air in summer and warm the air in winter. This can bring extra rain and snow to Michigan.

## Further Evidence

Look at the website below. Does it give any new evidence to support Chapter One?

## Michigan

abdocorelibrary.com/discovering -michigan

The Little River Band of Ottawa Indians hosts an annual powwow in Manistee, Michigan. The event features traditional dancing and music.

# CHAPTER 2

# The People of Michigan

The first people in Michigan arrived more than 11,000 years ago. Over time, different American Indian cultures developed. The Hopewell people lived in Michigan until 400 CE. They grew corn and hunted for food.

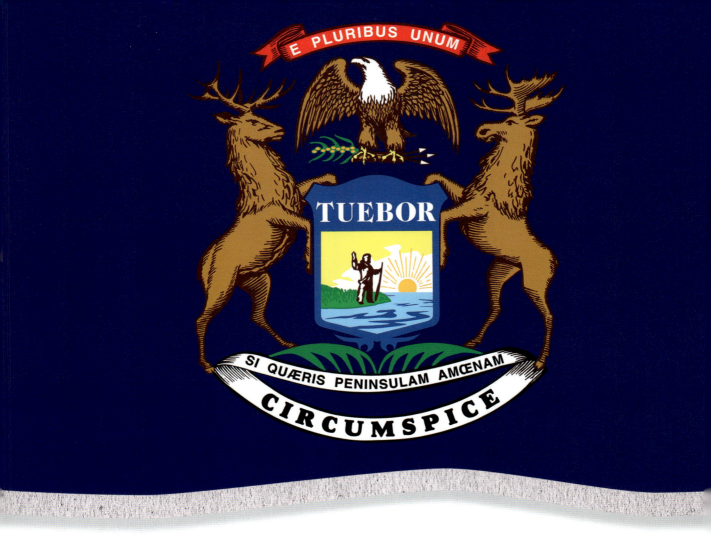

Michigan's state flag features an eagle, elk, and moose. It includes several Latin phrases, including one that means "If you seek a pleasant peninsula, look about you."

The Ottawa, Ojibwe, and Potawatomi peoples are native to Michigan too. They were there when European settlers arrived in the 1600s.

These three nations formed an **alliance** called the Three Fires. American Indians and European settlers traded goods. Other times, they fought over the land.

More white settlers came to Michigan in the 1800s. Many came from New York. Other **immigrants** were German, Irish, or Dutch.

In 2022, 74 percent of people in Michigan were white. Fourteen percent were Black, and 6 percent were Hispanic or Latino. Four percent were Asian. One percent were American Indian.

Some famous people come from Michigan. Businessman Henry Ford was born in the state in 1863. He started the Ford Motor Company in 1903. The company built and sold the Model T, one of the first successful US cars.

Henry Ford, *left*, worked with his son, Edsel, *right*. They both served as presidents of Ford Motor Company. Between 1908 and 1927, the company made 15 million Model T cars.

# Culture

Michigan's culture can be seen in its food. Immigrants from Cornwall brought Cornish pasties to the state. Cornwall is a region in the southwestern United Kingdom. Cornish pasties are meat pies stuffed with beef and vegetables. Bumpy cake is also popular. It was invented in the early 1900s. It features chocolate cake with frosting over vanilla buttercream bumps.

The city of Detroit is known for its music. Many **genres** of music are made there. These genres include jazz, rock, and blues.

# Industry

Many people in Michigan have jobs **manufacturing** cars, machines, and metal products. Since the 1900s, people in the state have depended on car companies for work.

## Motown Records

In 1959, Berry Gordy Jr. founded the company Motown Records in Detroit. It publishes music. In the 1960s, it released successful records in the soul music genre. Motown helped make many Black musicians famous, including Diana Ross and Marvin Gaye.

Michigan has the highest number of vehicle manufacturing workers in the country.

Michigan is home to several major car companies, including Ford and General Motors. The industry provides many jobs. Other people in Michigan farm crops or raise animals. Some workers cut down trees to make **lumber**.

Neal E. Boudette is a reporter from Michigan. He described how important cars are to the state, especially in Detroit:

> Detroit is Motor City. The whole region has this very strong connection to automobiles. There's a century-long history and a great deal of culture built around the automobile.

Source: Emmett Lindner. "A Changing Auto Industry, but Still 'Good Stories in Detroit.'" *New York Times*, 29 Sept. 2023, nytimes.com. Accessed 29 Sept. 2023.

## What's the Big Idea?

What is this quote's main idea? Explain how the main idea is supported by details.

Downtown Detroit is home to a mix of modern and historical buildings. It also has several popular riverfront parks, such as Hart Plaza.

# CHAPTER 3

# Places in Michigan

The capital of Michigan is Lansing. But Detroit is the state's largest city. It is on the Lower Peninsula. Other large cities include Grand Rapids and Ann Arbor. Marquette is the largest city on the Upper Peninsula.

# Parks

Michigan is home to several national parks. Isle Royale National Park is on an island in Lake Superior. Visitors take boats or planes to get there. They can camp and hike in the park's forests. Pictured Rocks National Lakeshore is on Lake Superior's southern shore. It features beautiful rock cliffs lining the water's edge.

Michigan also has many state parks. Ludington State Park is on Lake Michigan's eastern shore. People fish and ride boats there. At Tahquamenon Falls State Park, visitors can see waterfalls on the Tahquamenon River. The falls make the water foamy. People can also visit Porcupine Mountains Wilderness State Park.

Pictured Rocks National Lakeshore is known for its colorful cliffsides and unique rock formations. One popular sight is a natural rock arch called Lovers' Leap.

Tahquamenon Falls has two waterfalls, the Upper Falls and the Lower Falls. The Upper Falls is Michigan's largest waterfall. It is 200 feet (61 m) wide and 50 feet (15 m) tall.

It is Michigan's largest state park. It features forests, hiking trails, and scenic views.

# Landmarks

The Mackinac Bridge is a famous Michigan landmark. It connects the Upper and Lower Peninsulas. It opened in 1957. North of the bridge are the Soo Locks. These are a set of **canals**.

## Mackinac Island

Mackinac Island is a small island in Lake Huron. It is home to Mackinac Island State Park, where people can go camping. There is also a big hotel there. No cars are allowed on the island. People walk, ride bikes, or ride in horse-pulled carriages. Mackinac Island is famous for the fudge that is made there.

The Mackinac Bridge is more than 8,600 feet (2,600 m) long. It is one of the world's longest suspension bridges.

They allow boats to pass between Lake Superior and Lake Huron. The Soo Locks are important because many goods are transported on ships passing between the lakes.

The Automotive Hall of Fame is in Dearborn, Michigan. It is a museum that celebrates important people in the history of cars, such as Henry Ford. It is located next to the Henry Ford Museum, which has more than 100 vehicles on display.

Everybody can find something fun to do in Michigan. People can enjoy its beautiful parks. They can eat tasty desserts in Detroit. Or they can learn about the state's fascinating history.

## Explore Online

Visit the website below. Does it give any new information about Isle Royale National Park that wasn't in Chapter Three?

### Isle Royale National Park

abdocorelibrary.com/discovering -michigan

# State Map

## KEY

 Capital

 Park

City or town

Point of interest

Mackinac Island

Detroit

Pictured Rocks
National Lakeshore

# Michigan: The Wolverine State

Isle Royale National Park

Quincy Mine

Porcupine Mountain Wilderness State Park

Lake Superior

CANADA

Marquette

Tahquamenon Falls State Park

Soo Locks

Pictured Rocks National Lakeshore

Mackinac Bridge

Mackinac Island

Lake Huron

Houghton Lake

Ludington State Park

Muskegon River

Wisconsin

Grand Rapids

Lansing

Grand River

Lake Michigan

Detroit

Automotive Hall of Fame

Ann Arbor

Lake Erie

Illinois

Indiana

Ohio

N
W    E
S

# Glossary

**alliance**
an agreement between people or groups to work together

**canals**
human-made waterways that allow ships to pass between bodies of water

**genre**
a grouping of artwork made in a similar style

**immigrants**
people who move to a different country

**lumber**
logs used as building material

**manufacturing**
making goods to sell

**peninsula**
an area of land surrounded by water on three sides

# Online Resources

To learn more about Michigan, visit our free resource websites below.

Visit **abdocorelibrary.com** or scan this QR code for free Common Core resources for teachers and students, including vetted activities, multimedia, and booklinks, for deeper subject comprehension.

Visit **abdobooklinks.com** or scan this QR code for free additional online weblinks for further learning. These links are routinely monitored and updated to provide the most current information available.

# Learn More

Murray, Julie. *Michigan*. Abdo, 2020.

Ryan, Todd. *Michigan Wolverines*. Abdo, 2021.

Siber, Kate. *50 Adventures in the 50 States*. Wide Eyed Editions, 2020.

# Index

# About the Author

Ib Larsen is a writer and editorial assistant living in Saint Paul, Minnesota.